The Easi...
Learning Tho...

:S OF

...SION

...works.

the s...
SUCCESS
why not you?

2. **Prepare. Then prepare again.**

3. **Listen and watch.**

4. **Scarcity pushes people to act.**

"The Skinny on S...
funny, insightful a...
explanation as to...
people achieve ...
as good as it gets...

Jeffrey Kindler, CE(...

...to be

...e of

the skin...
willpo...
how...
sel...

"A Very Enjoyable Read!"

...lysis,
...ke
...ch

.../
...ties,
...gures.

"Don't let the stic...
fool you ... Jim F...
have you laughi...
thinking at the same time.
A very enjoyable read!"

Ken Blanchard, author
The One Minute Manager®

...all
...s.

...s is

www.theskinnyon.com

D0868956

...om

The Skinny on The Art of Persuasion

the skinny on™
the art of persuasion
how to move minds

Jim Randel

ISBN: 978-0-9824390-0-5
Ebook ISBN: 978-0-9841393-5-4
Library of Congress: 2010922321

Illustration/Design: Lindy Nass
Rebecca Kunzmann

For information address RAND Publishing, 265 Post Road West,
Westport, CT, 06880 or call (203) 226-8727.

The Skinny On™ books are available for special promotions and premiums.
For details contact: Donna Hardy, call (203) 222-6295 or visit our website:
www.theskinnyon.com

Printed in the United States of America

9 2 5 – 4 9 1 9
10 9 8 7 6 5 4 3 2

the skinny on™

Welcome to a new series of publications entitled **The Skinny On™,** a progression of drawings, dialogue and text intended to convey information in a concise and entertaining fashion.

In our time-starved and information-overloaded culture, most of us have far too little time to read. As a result, our understanding of important subjects often tends to float on the surface – without the insights of writings from thinkers and teachers who have spent years studying these subjects.

Our series is intended to address this situation. Our team of readers and researchers has done a ton of homework preparing our books for you. We read everything we could find on the topic at hand and spoke with the experts. Then we mixed in our own experiences and distilled what we have learned into this "skinny" book for your benefit.

Our goal is to do the reading for you, identify what is important, distill the key points, and present them in a book that is both instructive and enjoyable to read.

Although minimalist in design, we do take our message very seriously. Please do not confuse format with content. The time you invest reading this book will be paid back to you many, many times over.

"There are millions of words written about how the human brain works ... one thing is for sure. In order to persuade someone else to your way of thinking, you must align your mind with theirs. Successful persuasion begins and ends when there is a 'mind meld' of real meaning, feeling, and understanding.

So how do we establish this mind meld? ... The answer lies in understanding what motivates and drives the other person. Armed with that knowledge, you can position your thoughts and requests in such a way that they are easily and quickly accepted ... with little or no questioning."

Covert Persuasion: Psychological Tactics and Tricks to Win the Game,
Kevin Hogan and James Speakman (Wiley, 2006)

INTRODUCTION

Persuasion: *the act of convincing, influencing, or inducing.*

Great persuaders – people who can get into your brain and massage your cerebrum. Wow! What is more powerful than that?

Our team here at *The Skinny On* has studied great persuaders going back hundreds of years. And we have learned that persuasiveness is an acquired skill ... that there are principles, techniques, and strategies that you can develop to boost your persuasive powers.

The book you are holding will help you improve your persuasiveness. And if you can persuade others to your point of view – if you can move minds – well then you can do just about anything. In fact, in almost every endeavor in life, the more persuasive you are, the more likely you will be successful.

So, give us an hour of your time. We assure you that it will be one of the best hours you've ever spent!

FOREWORD

In this book I use the expression "persuasive event."

A persuasive event is any opportunity you have to influence another person's thinking. It can, of course, be a face-to-face meeting, but it does not have to be. It may be a letter, a phone call, an e-mail or text. Any form of communication with another person can be a persuasive event.

People in all walks of life are constantly engaged in persuasive events. Whoever you are and whatever you do, it's critical to be able to convince others to see your point of view.

BY THE END OF THIS BOOK, YOU WILL HAVE A GREATER APPRECIATION FOR THE GENIUS OF TOM SAWYER.

The Adventures of Tom Sawyer, Mark Twain

Hi, I'm Jim Randel and I'll be your moderator for our story. Throughout this book I'll be trying to influence your thinking – to persuade you to adopt some of my thoughts on the art of persuasion.

1

MEET BILLY AND BETH, THE HEROES OF OUR STORY. THEY ARE RECENTLY MARRIED.

Billy is 28 years old. He makes his living as a real estate broker.

Beth is 25. She works as a paralegal during the day and goes to law school at night.

2

"Yes, I know that … by the way, you look very nice this morning. It's just that she's so obvious and yet her phone rings off the hook."

"Could it be something you are doing wrong?"

5

"No … *it's not me!*"

6

Let's stop right here for a moment. Billy is wrong. _It is him_!

1. If Billy is not achieving what he wants, his first stop should be the mirror.

If Billy is not selling as well as others in his office, he needs to make a realistic assessment of why he is falling short. Every one of us can learn to be more persuasive.

2. Billy is wasting time criticizing Mary Johnson.

Mary is making sales and Billy is not. Billy should analyze what she is doing that he is not … and consider changing his approach.

It's time for me to introduce myself to Billy. I'm going to try to show him how to improve his persuasiveness.

At least I'm doing well at poker.

"Yes?"

KNOCK, KNOCK.

Billy

"Are you nuts?

"I am **_not_** pushy!!"

"I'll be going now, Billy."

17

I realize my approach to Billy was a bit aggressive. That was deliberate. My conduct mimicked Billy's approach to his business… he can be pushy ... and short with people when they don't see things his way.

In fact, he is constantly violating the #1 Rule of Persuasion.

18

RULE OF PERSUASION #1:

PEOPLE ARE PERSUADED BY PEOPLE THEY LIKE.

Rule #1 is so very basic – and yet many people ignore or forget it.

The fact is that all of us feel more trusting of and open to people we like ... people that seem similar to us.

"The more we feel connected to, part of, liked by, or attracted to someone, the more persuasive they become."

Maximum Influence: The 12 Universal Laws of Power Persuasion,
Kurt W. Mortensen (Amacom, 2004)

Great persuaders know how to build a connection with the people they are trying to persuade. They know how to put the other person at ease – how to lower his defenses:

1. They find a commonality – they identify some place or event or time that ties them to the other person. Once a mini-bond is created, it can be built upon.

2. They show interest and warmth – they ask questions about the other person. They solicit his or her viewpoints.

3. They are appreciative of the other person's qualities. Billy thinks that Mary Johnson is an insincere flatterer. And maybe she does overdo it, but the fact is that people love to hear nice things about themselves.

4. They adopt the vocabulary, tonality and speech patterns of the other person. Great persuaders are chameleon-like, they learn to adjust their persona to match up with other people. This puts the other person at ease.

The Journal of Experimental Social Psychology, Vol. 39 (2003) reports a study that emphasizes the importance of building a bond.

• • • • • • • • • •

Researchers in Holland wanted to observe the importance of familiarity … and then try to place a value on it. So they set up an experiment with waitresses at a popular restaurant.

23

One group of waitresses was instructed to repeat certain words in a customer's order **verbatim**. So when a customer said "bier" or "friet" (fries), the waitress would hesitate a few seconds and then repeat the order **using the exact word** "bier" or "friet."

The other group was also told to acknowledge the order but instead of using the exact words the customer used, the waitress would **use a synonym** for "bier" (e.g., "pils") or "friet" (e.g., "patat").

24

The researchers wanted to know whether there was a value to mirroring another's exact wording. Their theory was that there would be – that imitation in word choice would create some kind of bond between customer and waitress.

And the results were astounding: tips to the waitresses who repeated the customer's orders **verbatim** were **more than twice** those of the other waitresses.

25

"Imitation is the sincerest form of flattery."

Anonymous

26

The waitresses in the Dutch experiment had no idea what the objective of the exercise was. They treated all customers the same – the only point of distinction was how the customer's order was acknowledged.

And the experiment confirmed what the researchers had assumed: that even small differences in how you connect with people can lead to large differences in how they perceive you. The Dutch customers were obviously more comfortable with waitresses who used the **same words** as they did. And, they rewarded this comfort with much higher tips!!

For a comprehensive book on how to create a bond between you and the person you want to influence, try **The Magic of Rapport**, Richardson and Margulis (Hearst, 1981).

This book details ideas for creating rapport – the premise being that the more comfortable a person is with you, the more likely he or she will see things your way.

As an example, the authors speak to **pacing**, a term from the field of hypnosis. The authors suggest that by mirroring another person's rate of speech, tonality, volume and vocabulary, you lull them into thinking you are just like them.

"(Pacing) is being or becoming like other people so that you can get their attention and friendship and help."

ARE WE TALKING ABOUT MANIPULATION??

At times there is a fine line between manipulation and persuasion.

Some commentators feel that the difference is one of the persuader's intent.

"Manipulation is inwardly focused on the outcome for the person doing the manipulation. Persuasion is externally focused on developing a win-win outcome where everyone's needs are met."

Persuasion: The Art of Getting What You Want
Dave Lakhani, (Wiley, 2005)

I believe that the difference between manipulation and persuasion is in the nature of your approach.

To me, manipulation suggests an attempt to influence one's thoughts **using artificial or fraudulent means**. When I suggest you create a connection with another person, I don't propose you disguise your true self. You still must be **you**. You just try to access and display those parts of **you** that are going to be most familiar to the other person.

If you attempt to alter your essence in an effort to influence someone else's thinking, he or she will most likely see through you anyway.

31

"Just like you, I go to church every Sunday, I volunteer at the soup kitchen, I read poetry, I do yoga."

Could this guy be any more transparent? Who is he trying to fool??

32

We can't leave the subject of manipulation without introducing a man named Niccolo Machiavelli. Machiavelli lived from 1469 to 1527. He wrote a well-known book titled *The Prince*.

The Prince was Machiavelli's analysis of how rulers gained and maintained power. Machiavelli believed that rulers needed to use manipulation and duplicity. Today the word "Machiavellian" means an approach characterized by craftiness and expediency.

We here at *The Skinny On* feel that it is our job to bring you all sides of important topics. Some people believe that Machiavelli was correct. Others think that disingenuous people are eventually discovered and never achieve long-term success.

Our point of view is the latter. The rulers in Machiavelli's day (500 years ago) lived in a world connected by word of mouth. Truth and reputation spread slowly. Today, one serious misstep on your part can be "heard" by others in minutes. And, once you obtain a reputation for insincerity, you will never be able to persuade people of anything.

We believe that to be a great persuader – and a good person – you need to use your persuasive skills in a decent and honorable fashion.

> *"The most important single ingredient in the formula of success is knowing how to get along with people."*

Teddy Roosevelt

BACK TO BILLY AND BETH

"So this jerk drops in on me today. Named Jim Randel. Tells me he wants to help me."

"About 6 feet tall? Very good looking?"

37

"Well I would *definitely* not call him good looking, but yes, he was about 6 feet tall … what kind of question is that anyway?"

"If it's the same guy, I've met him."

38

Dale Carnegie's book, **How to Win Friends and Influence People** was written in 1936. It has sold 20 million copies. Although 75 years old, this book still has tremendous relevance today.

"Why not study the technique of the greatest winner of friends the world has ever known? Who is he? You may meet him tomorrow coming down the street. When you get within ten feet of him, he will begin to wag his tail. If you stop and pet him, he will almost jump out of his skin to show you how much he likes you. And you know that behind this show of affection on his part, there are no ulterior motives: he doesn't want to sell you any real estate, and he doesn't want to marry you."

How to Win Friends and Influence People,
Dale Carnegie (Prentice Hall, 1936)

Carnegie is not really suggesting you act like a puppy in order to win people over. He is using the puppy example as a metaphor. His point is that people will lower their defenses when approached by a person who shows pleasure to see them ... who expresses warmth with no apparent ulterior motive ... who has endearing qualities.

Here are Carnegie's five suggestions for winning people over:

    (1) smile
    (2) show interest in the other person
    (3) encourage the other to talk about him or herself
    (4) make the other person feel important
    (5) pay close attention to what the other is saying.

This stuff certainly isn't rocket science. Still, it's incredible how many people (like Billy) miss opportunities to connect with others.

Dale Carnegie was a genius at understanding people.

But the point I want to make is this: the challenge is not just **to appear** warm, gracious and interested. The challenge is **to be** warm, gracious and interested.

I believe that the best persuaders are people who are actually interested in other people. Who connect with others not just because they need to – in order to persuade – but because they want to. If you are someone who "couldn't care less," you will never be a great persuader. Nor much of a person.

"The senior partner in our law firm never pays attention to the paralegals, and so ..."

*I wonder how my fantasy football team did ... **Uh oh**, I think Beth is talking to me.*

47

Billy is not a very good listener. He is also tone deaf in that he doesn't hear or see himself the way others do.

I have my work cut out for me with Billy. But we'll get back to him. Let's move on to the second rule for effective persuasion.

48

RULE OF PERSUASION #2:

PREPARE BEFORE YOU SPEAK.
THEN, PREPARE AGAIN.

An effective persuasion is not something that just happens. Most great persuaders – from salespeople to politicians to trial attorneys – think about what they are trying to accomplish and how they are going to do that **well in advance of moving their lips**.

As it happens, I will be addressing this topic tonight during my course on persuasion at the law school.

Good evening. Tonight we are going to discuss the connection between persuasion and preparation. The probability that you will achieve a successful persuasive event is directly proportional to the amount of preparation you do **before you even start trying to persuade**.

51

Some people have the impression that great trial lawyers are silver-tongued orators with a natural ability to sway a judge or jury. That's not the fact. What sways people is a well-conceived, well-presented argument or position that makes sense to the listener. That is why the most successful trial lawyers spend hours and hours in preparation before they ever get to the courtroom.

52

The same is true for business attorneys. As negotiation is critical in any business deal, good business attorneys think through what they want to say in advance of meeting with the other party or attorney. Ditto for good salespeople. And so on.

The Art of Persuasion
Fall Semester

Professor Jim Randel

"The mark of the serious person, or the real professional, in any field is that he takes far more time to prepare than the average. ... Great successes are often determined by attention to the smallest details. One fact, one inaccuracy, can make all the difference. And everything counts."

**The 100 Absolutely Unbreakable
Laws of Business Success,**
Brian Tracy (BK Publishers, 2000)

Preparation is about scripting a persuasive event as much as possible.

There are three good reasons why preparation will improve your persuasiveness.

First, the more you prepare, the more comfortable you will be in your presentation.

When you are prepared, you will be more at ease during your presentation. And a listener can sense that. When you are unprepared, you may be stressed and the other person can sense that too. The more comfortable you are, the more comfortable the listener is, and the higher the probability that she will decide as you wish.

1. COMFORT
2. CONTROL
3. SILENCE

The second reason preparation works is that the better prepared you are, the more control you will exercise over the listener's thought processes.

You should assume that no matter how interesting you are, your listener's mind is flitting around. That is human nature. Your goal is to keep control of the other person's attention as best you can.

1. COMFORT
2. CONTROL
3. SILENCE

During your preparation, you need to consider where you may lose the other person's attention. If there is a progression to your presentation that the listener must follow, think through where the chain might break.

Reflect on how to keep the listener focused on the logic and sequence of your presentation. Prepare for those times when his mind may wander from or reject what you are saying.

I have always been interested in magic. When performing magic, especially close-up magic like card or coin tricks, a magician learns the importance of controlling his audience. These tricks usually involve sleight of hand, and so one of the goals of the magician is to distract the viewer from seeing exactly what he is doing.

This distraction – or what magicians call misdirection – is about controlling the mind and eyes of the audience. It involves a lot of practice and preparation.

"Misdirection is part of this psychological technique (of magicians). It is the science of controlling not only the spectators' eyes, but also their minds. It is this phase of magic that attracts so many doctors, lawyers, teachers, and other people who have a particular interest in the way the human mind works. I once heard a psychiatrist – who was also an excellent card trickster say that through his attention to misdirection, the magician develops a knowledge of certain peculiarities of human thought that surpasses anything to be found in psychology books."

How to Do Tricks with Cards,
Bill Turner (Collier Books, 1949)

The third reason to prepare is to reflect upon what you can reasonably accomplish in a given persuasive event. This helps you decide when to stop talking and let silence create its impact.

Does this seem odd to you?

Do you really have to spend time preparing to know exactly when to shut up?

Well, let me give you a three-part answer: YES! YES!! YES!!!

Most people love the sound of their own voice. When they are talking – and especially when things are going well for them – they get caught up in the moment. They want to talk forever. Unfortunately, that can have a negative effect.

I want to tell you a story told to me many years ago by a law professor of mine. His name was Irving. Before he was a professor he was a trial lawyer.

One day Irving was in his office when a man came to see him with a big bandage where his nose should have been. The man claimed that he had been in a fight, and that the other guy had bitten off his nose.

"I want to sue the guy!"

After doing some homework, Irving decided to take the case and it went to trial.

The defendant claimed that he had not bitten off the nose … that it had been sliced off when Irving's client fell against some glass. Irving knew that a jury would award greater damages to his client if they concluded that the defendant had in fact bitten off his client's nose.

There was only one witness to the fight. His name was Smith. Irving had prepared well. He knew what Smith would say. Unfortunately for the defendant, his attorney was not as well prepared.

Smith is on the stand being questioned by the defendant's attorney.

"So, Mr. Smith, given where you were located, you could not possibly have seen my client bite off the plaintiff's nose ... is that not correct?"

"Yes, that's correct."

65

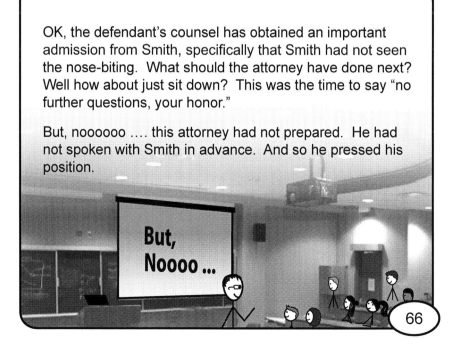

OK, the defendant's counsel has obtained an important admission from Smith, specifically that Smith had not seen the nose-biting. What should the attorney have done next? Well how about just sit down? This was the time to say "no further questions, your honor."

But, noooooo .... this attorney had not prepared. He had not spoken with Smith in advance. And so he pressed his position.

But,
Noooo ...

66

Irving **really enjoyed** that moment.

He knew what Smith would say. And he knew that he could elicit the full story when it was his chance to question Smith.

But, when the defendant's own counsel brought forth the incriminating information … well, that was so juicy (no pun intended).

The defendant's attorney had never learned the key to effective (persuasive) cross-examination... **methodical preparation**.

Preparation forces you to think through what you can accomplish in a given persuasive event, and when to stop pressing.

Excuse me for getting worked up, but people who don't know when to quit talking drive me nuts!

If you want to be an effective persuader, you must know when to stop pushing. I can't count the times I've been in a courtroom, or business negotiation, or sales presentation when a persuader hurt himself by not knowing when to shut the heck up.

"When you strike 'ile' (oil), stop boring; many a man has bored clean through and let the 'ile' run out of the bottom!"

Advice from a famous Scottish trial attorney

The Art of Cross-Examination,
Francis Wellman (McMillian, 1903)

73

In recap then, there are three good reasons to prepare **before** you attempt to persuade:

One, the more prepared you are, the more fluid you will be.

Two, the better your preparation, the stronger your control over the listener.

Three, with preparation, you will know precisely when to stop pushing.

Let's now move on to my next important Rule of Persuasion.

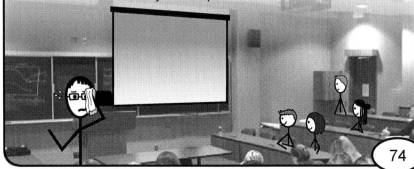

74

RULE OF PERSUASION #3:
LEARN TO LISTEN AND WATCH.

Are you enjoying the book so far? I hope so.

It never ceases to amaze me how many really good speakers are such poor listeners.

If you want to be a good persuader, you must teach yourself to be a good listener.

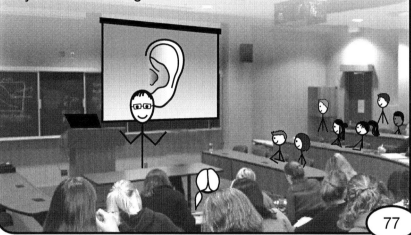

There are at least three reasons why listening and persuasiveness are directly related:

1. People like people who listen to them. We have already learned that the more someone likes you, the more likely you will be able to persuade him to your point of view.

2. When you listen, you pick up clues. If you are really attentive, you will hear and see tips as to what the other person is thinking.

3. When you listen, your mind quiets and your creativity increases. A focused listener shuts off distractions and concentrates her energy – as a result her mind is nimble and fluid.

I have thought a lot about listening. I think it is one of the most important skills you can develop. A good listener can create an instant bond with another person. A bad listener can create instant animosity.

"Unfortunately, few people are good listeners. Even at the purely informational level, researchers claim that 75% of oral communication is ignored, misunderstood or quickly forgotten. Rarer still is the ability to listen for the deepest meanings in what people say. How devastating, but how common, to talk with someone about subjects of intense interest to oneself only to experience the stifling realization that the other person was not really listening ..."

People Skills, Robert Bolton
(Touchstone Books, 1979)

79

In addition to training yourself to be a good listener, you might want to learn more about body language. There are many good books on the subject. One that I just finished reading is **The Definitive Book of Body Language** by Allan and Barbara Pease.

Body Language

80

"We all, in one way or another, send our little messages out to the world ... And rarely do we send our messages consciously. We act out our state of being with nonverbal body language. We lift one eyebrow for disbelief. We rub our noses for puzzlement. We clasp our arms to isolate ourselves or protect ourselves. We shrug our shoulders for indifference, wink one eye for intimacy, tap our fingers for impatience, slap our foreheads for forgetfulness. The gestures are numerous, and while some are deliberate, there are some, such as rubbing our noses for puzzlements or clasping our arms to protect ourselves, that are mostly unconscious."

Body Language, Julius Fast
(Pocket Books, 1971)

81

Want to be a strong persuader?

Think **big ears** ... **big eyes** ... **small mouth**.

82

And here's another suggestion about listening:

If you want to improve your persuasive skills, listen to YOURSELF.

Sometimes when I prepare for a persuasive event, I imagine that I am stepping out of my body, and I play the role of the person on the other side of the table.

The virtual me then listens to my presentation.

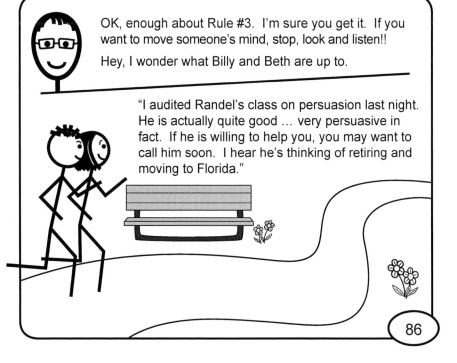

Perhaps without even realizing it, Beth is persuading Billy to call me by using our next Rule of Persuasion.

Gee, maybe I'd better call him.

RULE OF PERSUASION #4:

SCARCITY –

PEOPLE WANT WHAT THEY CAN'T HAVE.

"Whenever choice is limited or threatened, the human need to maintain a share of the limited commodity makes us crave it even more. Scarcity increases the value of any product or service. Scarcity drives people to action, making us act quickly for fear of missing out on an opportunity."

Maximum Influence, Kurt W. Mortensen

It's pretty cold here in Connecticut today. This fire sure feels good. Beth is right … I am thinking of retiring to Florida.

Anyway, as to the 4th Rule of Persuasion, if you want to convince someone to act, you need to create a line around their choices. Sometimes the line is the number of choices, sometimes it is a finite time period, sometimes it is the exclusivity of the offering.

Let me give you an example of how innate the law of scarcity is.

A few years ago psychologists did a study with young children.

They brought children into a room divided with a low plexiglass barrier. There were toys on both sides of the plexiglass. The children were tall enough to reach over the plexiglass barrier if they wanted to. In this situation, the children showed no preference for the toys on the far side of the barrier.

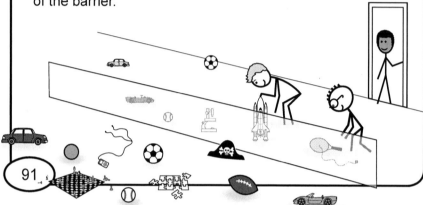

91

Then, a few days later, the psychologists set the same scenario – same children, same toys – **but this time they raised the height** of the plexiglass. Now it was too high for the children to get to the toys on the other side. The result?

In this situation the children showed a strong preference for the toys on the far side of the plexiglass.

In other words, they wanted what they could not have! Human nature, I tell you … human nature!!

92

Smart marketers understand that people want what they can't have. For this reason they create scarcities when trying to persuade someone to act. Sometimes the scarcities are legitimate, sometimes not.

93

DO ANY OF THESE SOUND FAMILIAR??

"For a limited time only."

"While supplies last."

"By invitation only."

"Going out of business sale."

"Only available from our company."

94

Billy's co-worker, Mary Johnson, understands the law of scarcity.

"I'm glad you like this house. I thought you would. It is in many ways **one of a kind**. Why don't you sleep on things before making an offer? However, I suggest you call me tomorrow if you can. This house is priced correctly and probably **won't be on the market for too long.**"

For Sale

95

Billy, too, is aware of the law of scarcity. He, however, has never looked up the word "subtlety" in the dictionary.

"Wow, what a great house!! Glad you like it. Tell you the truth I would not be surprised if another agent with buyers **drives up the minute we leave**. We have **got to act fast** or we'll **lose this house** to other buyers!"

For Sale

96

As with many things in life, success is a matter of degree. Billy does understand that sometimes a seller must create a sense of urgency to get buyers to act. **But**, he has no sense of proportion. He puts down the pedal **all the way, all the time**.

Please note that the title of this book is *The Skinny on The Art of Persuasion*.

Good persuaders understand that persuasiveness is an art ... that to be effective, they must have a sense of dimension and, of nuance. If you push people too hard, they will instinctively pull back.

I have studied the subject of persuasion for many years. I have been an observer of great persuaders … and of terrible ones. And I have found one consistent difference between the great and the terrible.

The great ones sell with nuance and finesse. They respect the intelligence of the other person.

The terrible ones oversell. They underestimate how perceptive most people are.

99

To be a great persuader you must think before you speak. You must learn to put several beats between what you are thinking, and what you are saying. You must train yourself to reflect on the impact of what you will say – **before** you say it.

Many people neglect to censor their thoughts. They just start speaking and twaddle on and on. These people are almost always ineffective persuaders.

100

Before I was a law professor, I was a practicing attorney. I was involved in many negotiations, and sometimes my job was to keep my client in check ... to help him think before speaking. That was not always easy. Let me give you an example.

101

Several years ago I was representing a man who had just built a large office building. His broker had done a good job and had identified a company interested in leasing the entire building. My client asked the CEO of that company and her attorney to come to a meeting at his office. He hoped to persuade the CEO to agree to lease his building.

102

My client did a good job explaining to the CEO the advantages of his building. And he outlined for her the terms of a lease agreement he felt would be attractive ... The CEO reacted favorably.

"Mr. Building Owner, your terms are fair and I appreciate your outlining them so clearly. I don't need time to think this over. I'm sure we will be very happy in your building."

103

OK, what should my client have said next? "Great" would be nice ... or, "I look forward to your first day in our building." Instead, he just starts blabbing.

"That's great, Ms. CEO. We do believe we have the nicest building in town and the silliness that's going around about our parking is just ridiculous."

104

All of a sudden the discussion started going south. The CEO never thought parking was a problem. But now, with my client bringing it up, she started to ask questions.

"Is parking a problem?"

"Oh no … I've just heard that some of the brokers are saying it is. But, <u>no</u>, <u>no</u>, <u>no</u> … parking is no problem!"

Why can't he learn to think <u>before</u> he speaks?

Once my client brought up parking, the CEO became concerned.

And none of this needed to occur. My client's building had an undeserved bad rap about parking. In fact, he was correct – there was no problem. BUT, because he did not think before speaking, the deal was in jeopardy. Fortunately, after several more weeks of negotiation, the deal went through.

"Always put your mind in gear BEFORE you take your mouth out of park!"

Anonymous

GOOD NEWS:

I'M ABOUT TO HEAR FROM BILLY.

"Hello ... Billy ... how nice to hear from you. Sure, I would love to have lunch with you."

I'm glad Billy called. I have some suggestions for him. And I'm going to introduce him to Rule of Persuasion #5.

RULE OF PERSUASION #5:

PEOPLE STRIVE TO REMAIN CONSISTENT WITH PREVIOUSLY MADE STATEMENTS OR COMMITMENTS.

"Billy, success with sales, success with any effort to persuade another, is a skill you can develop.

As an example, in order to be an effective persuader, you need to understand how people process information and make decisions."

"I do understand people, Jim."

"No, Billy, you understand **some** people. You understand people who decide like you do… I know that you are an impulse buyer. You are quick to make a decision and, you often rely on just your gut.

Am I close?"

"Yes, that is an accurate description of me."

113

"OK, well there is nothing wrong with that but it's not how everyone decides.

Many people are much more methodical and deliberative than you are. I'm afraid you often make the mistake of **confusing the familiar with the universal.**"

"HUH??"

114

"Billy, to some extent we all assume that other people see the world, process information and make decisions exactly the way we do. We confuse the **familiar**, our way of doing things, with the **universal**, how other people do things. When we make that mistake, we approach situations as if the other party thinks and acts like we do."

"Ahhh … I get that."

"OK, good.

Now, at the same time, there are some rules that apply across the board. One of the most important of these is the rule of consistency – that people tend to stay true to a perception they have of themselves.

Let me give you an example. … Oh wait, just before I do that I want you to know that I am giving a seminar on persuasive skills tomorrow night. There is one opening left. Would you like to attend?"

"Well, I'd like to know a little bit more about it."

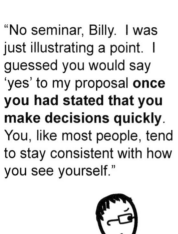

"No seminar, Billy. I was just illustrating a point. I guessed you would say 'yes' to my proposal **once you had stated that you make decisions quickly**. You, like most people, tend to stay consistent with how you see yourself."

"So you deliberately backed me into a corner when I indicated my preference for immediate decisions … and then tricked me into making an immediate decision?"

119

"Pretty much, yes. Let me tell you about some fascinating research."

This guy needs a life.

120

Years ago, a group of researchers went into a California neighborhood and asked homeowners for permission to place a huge sign in their front yards. The sign said "DRIVE CAREFULLY." Because the sign was so large, almost all the homeowners said "no."

"Sorry, no."

Then the researchers shifted gears. In a similar neighborhood they asked homeowners whether they would display a small sign in the window of their house. The sign said "Be a Safe Driver." Most of the homeowners said "sure."

Three weeks later, researchers went back into the neighborhood and asked whether they could replace the small window sign with a huge "DRIVE CAREFULLY" sign in homeowners' front yards. **This time, 76% said "yes!"**

What had happened? Well, at the time the homeowners were asked about the large sign, they had previously made a commitment to safe driving (displaying the small sign). The large-sign request was just a logical extension of how these homeowners now perceived themselves (safe-driving advocates).

We all like to think of ourselves as consistent creatures. Once we make a commitment or perceive ourselves in a certain way, we struggle to remain true to our commitment or perception.

123

"You mean just by accepting a small sign in their window promoting safe driving, these people were later vulnerable to the big-sign pitch?"

124

"Yes, Billy, once people take a stand, they tend to stay consistent with that position."

"Hmmm."

125

People's desire to remain consistent with positions they have taken reveals itself in a variety of situations.

One study indicated that people who bet at horse races are much more confident about their bet **immediately after they make it**. Once they take a stand, their uncertainty goes away!

Similarly, there is the principle of loss aversion. Many people who buy a stock that subsequently declines in price are reluctant to sell (even when all signs advocate for doing so). These people are trying to **remain true to the analysis they did and the stand they took** when they bought.

126

"If I can get you to make a commitment (that is, to take a stand, to go on record), I will have set the stage for your automatic ... consistency with that earlier commitment. Once a stand is taken, there is a natural tendency to behave in ways that are stubbornly consistent with that stand."

Influence: The Psychology of Persuasion,
Robert Cialdini (Harper Collins, 1984)

Sometimes even experts get stuck in the rule of consistency.

I love playing sports although when it comes to basketball I'm always the last guy chosen on pick-up teams. I'm a little hurt by this but realize that athletic talent is sometimes hard to see.

Did you know, for example, that in the 1984 NBA college draft the Portland Trail Blazers had the #2 choice and picked Sam Bowie over Michael Jordan? Who's Sam Bowie? That's my point!

I've heard of David Bowie ... but Sam??

129

The NBA draft is a huge guess-fest that takes place every year as professional teams try to identify future superstars. And, as you would expect, the higher a player goes in the draft, the more likely he will become a star. **But**, when two economists did an in-depth analysis of the NBA draft and a player's performance in the NBA, they found something very interesting.

What the economists learned is that the higher a player went in the draft, the more playing time he received. On its face, this would seem logical. But what the statistics showed is that **even when one player had better stats than another, what really counted in getting playing time was how high a player had been selected in the draft.**

130

You see once the experts – the coaches and team management – had made a draft choice, they felt committed to their decision. Even if a player picked in a lower position performed better, the teams gave more playing time to the higher-selected player.

I can handle this guy.

131

"(T)he variable most responsible for an NBA player's time on the court – 'above and beyond any effects of a player's performance, injury or trade status' – was his draft selection order."

Sway: The Irresistible Pull of Irrational Behavior,
Ori Brafman and Rom Brafman (Doubleday, 2008)

132

"Persuaders who ply people using the forces of consistency learn to influence in increments. They get a small commitment. Then they move that forward in gradual steps. Eventually they attempt to turn these small, incremental moves into a large decision in their favor."

"Sounds like the foot-in-the-door strategy."

"Yes, Billy. The foot-in-the-door technique is an example."

The foot-in-the-door technique is about getting people moving in the direction you want. By extracting minor commitments (the foot being in the door), you can often move someone forward to a major decision.

The foot-in-the door technique is also about inertia.

Inertia is a force of nature that states:

1. A body at rest will remain at rest unless acted upon by an outside force; and

2. A body in motion will remain in motion unless acted upon by an outside force.

Good persuaders know how to use inertia. Getting one's "foot in a door" is a way to put things in motion. And motion begets motion.

Another example of inertia in use is the fascinating study of **default options**.

Good persuaders understand that people are reluctant to make decisions – especially decisions that require some deliberation, introspection or analysis. This is an example of the first leg of inertia – a body at rest prefers to stay at rest.

So, smart marketers create default options – such that a **non-decision** triggers the marketer's preferred choice.

Let me give you an illustration.

States across the U.S. want to encourage drivers to become organ donors.

States have learned that if they ask people:

"Do you want to be an organ donor?"

a predictable (but smaller-than-desired) number will respond affirmatively.

So, some states took a different approach and asked:

"Do you want to be an organ donor? Unless you indicate 'no,' we will presume you mean 'yes.'"

Want to guess the impact? The number of people "consenting" to be organ donors increased dramatically.

THE POWER OF FORCING PEOPLE TO OPT-OUT

These states figured out how to use inertia in their favor. They put the onus on people "at rest" to make a decision – realizing that most people at rest will remain at rest. Then, they turned a **non-decision** into the choice the states wanted – effectively a decision in favor of organ donations.

Want to know how powerful inertia is? Well, take two similar countries – Germany and Austria. Germany requires people to **opt in** to organ donations and 12% of Germany's drivers have opted in. Austria requires people to **opt out** if they do not want to be donors. In Austria 99% of drivers are organ donors!!

"Many people will take whatever option requires the least effort, or the path of least resistance. ... if, for a given choice, there is a default option – an option that will obtain if the chooser does nothing – than we can expect a large number of people to end up with that option, whether it is good for them or not."

Nudge, Thaler and Sunstein (Penguin, 2008)

BACK TO JIM AND BILLY AT THE DINER

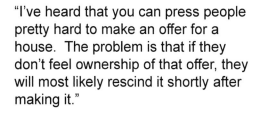

"I've heard that you can press people pretty hard to make an offer for a house. The problem is that if they don't feel ownership of that offer, they will most likely rescind it shortly after making it."

"That has happened to me a lot lately."

145

"Billy, the only 'yes' that counts is the 'yes' a person makes of his or her own volition."

"Maybe I do push too hard at times."

146

"Good persuaders learn that the way to persuade is **to guide** a person to make a commitment that she will thereafter wish to remain consistent with. The operative word is guide. He or she needs **to allow** your foot in the door – and not because you're pushing on the door with all your might."

147

"The professional salesperson never gives anyone the impression that he's pushing them – for the simple reason that he never pushes. But he does lead."

How to Master the Art of Selling,
Tom Hopkins (Warner, 1982)

148

OK, let's move on. Like the rule of consistency, there's another truism of human nature that can help you learn to persuade successfully. And that is our next Rule of Persuasion.

RULE OF PERSUASION #6:

PEOPLE DON'T LIKE TO FEEL INDEBTED.

Right now I'm engaged in a little game I've played for the last few holiday seasons.

Just for fun I go into the County tax rolls and randomly select 500 names of people I don't know. Then, I send them a holiday card which says:

"Seasons Greetings. Your neighbor, Jim Randel."

I first did this two years ago. And last year I got back 88 cards from people in return. People who had no clue who I was but who felt that since I had sent them a card, they should send me one. Cool, heh??

This year I'm going to send out 1,000 cards. It's kind of a silly game but no one gets hurt and I just love looking at pictures of people's families.

Anyway, my point is that people react predictably when they feel someone has done something for them. Specifically, they feel they should do something in return. This is sometimes called the rule of reciprocity: if you want to get someone to do something for you, do something for them first.

The rule of reciprocity plays on the discomfort people feel when they are under a sense of obligation. From the time you were a child, you were probably ingrained with a sense that if someone did something nice for you, you should do something nice back.

Smart persuaders learn how to take advantage of this reflex – and use it to their advantage.

153

As an example, some marketers use free samples as a way to create a sense of obligation.

When you receive a free sample, the marketer has two objectives:

First, she wants you to try her product ... and hopefully, like it.

But also second, she wants to create a desire to reciprocate – a feeling that since she did something nice for you (free sample), you should do something nice back in return (buy her products).

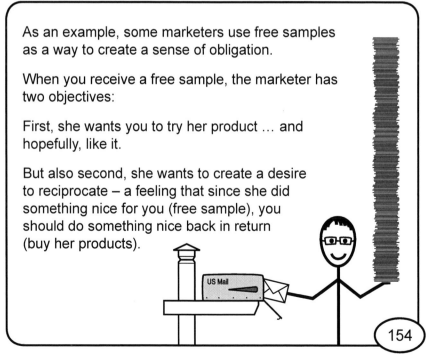

154

I recently read about an experiment in a Wisconsin supermarket where a cheese company gave away free samples for one week. Now Wisconsin is not a state where people are going to be easily convinced to buy a new brand of cheese. I doubt that the free cheese was that much better than other cheeses Wisconsin folks had tasted before.

But, you know what? After the week's free samples, shoppers in that store bought lots of the cheese company's products – in large part, researchers believe, because the free cheese created a sense of obligation in those who ate it.

US Mail

155

Personally, I don't like cheese. It gives me a stomach ache. But hey, people in Wisconsin, they love their Packers and they love their cheese. And just like people everywhere, they labor under a pressure of reciprocity. Do something for them and they will want to do something back in return.

Understanding reciprocity is important to being a good persuader and it leads me to another point: the **tempo** of a successful persuasion.

156

Great persuaders understand that there is often a tempo or rhythm to making a sale. Often a persuader needs to bide his or her time to convert or move someone's mind from A to B. People who try to rush things – who try to accelerate the pace of a persuasion – often fall flat.

As we have discussed, people cannot be pressured. They must come to the conclusion themselves that what is being suggested is what they want. This often takes time.

157

This is my wife, Carol. She is a beautiful woman who had no interest in me when I first pursued her. She thought I was some kind of geek...Imagine!!

Well, fortunately I had patience; I knew about the tempo of making a sale. And I understood the rule of reciprocity. I sent her lots of nice things to get her attention – flowers, candy, and the like. Eventually she felt sorry for me and agreed to a have a cup of coffee with me.

158

Not the best first impression. But I kept at it. It took me months but eventually she agreed to have dinner with me. I did not bring my stopwatch to dinner, by the way. We had a lovely dinner. She got to see that although a bit goofy, I'm really a nice guy. And, well, things took off from there.

You see, there is a time frame to every sale. A measured pace that must be adhered to. And sometimes by doing nice things for the person you want to persuade, you create a sense of obligation that will at least get his or her attention. Hopefully one thing will lead to another and you will be able to wed your objectives with the other person's desires.

Patience is, of course, a virtue.

• •

"Dear Lord, please grant me patience ... and I need it RIGHT NOW!!"

Anonymous

Well, I have to take a break now to get ready for my lecture at the law school this evening. But just before I do, let me have a little fun with you as a way to introduce my next rule of persuasion.

One way that magicians fool people is by taking advantage of the mental shortcuts people take. For example, when you have always experienced something proceeding from A to B and then B to C, you most likely think that is how it **always happens**.

Magicians know this and so they will sometimes switch up the order of what is really happening. The magician is relying on the fact that most people don't stop and question what they are watching. Magicians know that most of us simply make assumptions about what is happening.

I would now like to do a magic trick for you. Below are six cards.

Now select one of these cards. Think of nothing else but that card. Focus on it with all your might. Got it? OK, now I will perform my magic.

First, I will create a light mist.

Tap!
Tap!

Amazing, heh? How could I possibly have known the card you would select?

Think for a second.

Got it? Of course. I changed all six cards. No matter which card you focused on, it is not in the second group.

Did I catch you … at least for a few seconds?

Probably. And the reason is because my asking you to focus on one card caused you to think I would touch only one card. You **presumed** something that was not accurate.

By the way, I never lied to you. Please note my exact language: "the card you focused on is now missing." I never said I replaced only one card.

People tend to rely on shortcuts when making decisions.

They tend to reach decisions and conclusions without analyzing each step or component of a presentation, proposal or sales pitch.

RULE OF PERSUASION #7:

IN LIEU OF ANALYSIS, PEOPLE OFTEN TAKE SHORTCUTS TO REACH DECISIONS.

Good evening, students.

Tonight I am going to speak about the shortcuts people take when they do not have the time, expertise, or interest to make a careful analysis.

PEOPLE
TAKE
SHORTCUTS.

Please look at the drawing on the white screen. As you can see, there are two coffee tables. Please tell me which of the two is the longer and narrower.

Got it? OK, get ready to be surprised. Both tables are exactly the same size.

I know. It's fascinating to me too because they sure don't look that way. This is an optical illusion which is just another way of saying our minds can be fooled by how certain information is presented.

In a well-written book, **Nudge**, the authors make the point that our minds are divided into two functional parts. We use the **Automatic** system when we act out of reflex or instinct. We use the **Reflective** system when we sit back and think or analyze before making a choice or decision.

Because of the stresses and demands of coping with a highly complex world, we often rely on our Automatic system to make decisions for us.

Let me give you an example of how people react when they do not have the time or expertise to analyze a proposition.

There was a store in a tourist area with fine turquoise jewelry for sale – real high-quality products. **But** nothing was selling!

177

So the owner of the store decided to reduce his prices, and he sent his store manager an e-mail telling her to do that. **But** the store manager misread the e-mail and **thought she was supposed to double the prices**. Soon thereafter, the jewelry started selling like hot cakes.

178

What was going on? Well, the tourists had no idea what good turquoise jewelry should sell for. At the original prices, the jewelry seemed too inexpensive to be of top quality. So, the tourists did not buy.

But when the prices were accidentally doubled, people coming into the store **assumed** that given the high prices, the jewelry was of exceptional quality. And they got in line to buy.

PEOPLE EQUATE PRICE AND VALUE.

179

The tourists were not acting irrationally.

Most of the time, good quality products command high prices. In this situation, they had no ability to assess the value of the jewelry, so they fell back on a reliable shortcut in thinking.

180

Shrewd marketers (persuaders) understand that people often equate price with value.

Staying with a jewelry example, let me tell you about the black pearl.

In 1970, a well-known pearl merchant, Salvador Assael, was introduced to the black pearl. These pearls come from Tahitian oysters. But after much effort, Assael could not generate a demand for black pearls.

Until, that is, he hatched a plan (no pun intended). He went to a friend of his, jeweler Harry Winston, and asked if he could put a string of black pearls in Winston's storefront window – **with a very high price tag attached**. Winston said "yes," and before you could say "Tahitian oyster," strings of black pearls were appearing on the wealthiest female necks in New York City.

One of my favorite examples of how people fall prey to the price-quality presumption is an experiment performed by a Professor Baba Shiv of Stanford University.

Professor Shiv asked people to sample a new high-energy drink that was supposed to make them more alert (in actuality, sugar water). Some of the people were charged full price for the drink. Others were offered a discount. But, everybody got the same drink.

Then the sugar-water drinkers were given a set of puzzles to solve.

Here's the amazing result: **those who received the discounted drink consistently solved 30% fewer puzzles than those who paid in full.** In other words, the people who got the discounted "high-energy" drink figured they were getting a less-potent version and, their beliefs became their realities.

"We ran the study again and again, not sure if what we got had happened by chance or fluke ... But every time we ran it, we got the same results."

Professor Baba Shiv

"Why did the cheaper energy drink prove less effective? ... Since (people) expect cheaper goods to be less effective, they generally are less effective. That is why brand-name aspirin works better than generic aspiring and why Coke tastes better than cheaper colas, even if most consumers can't tell the difference in blind taste tests.

'We have these general beliefs about the world – for example, that cheaper products are of lower quality – and they translate into specific expectations about specific products,' said Shiv. 'Then, once these expectations are activated, they start to really impact our behavior.'"

How We Decide, Jonah Lehrer
(Houghton Mifflin, 2009)

In addition to playing on a price-equals-value reflex, some persuaders also call into use the principle of contrast.

The principle of contrast suggests that if I want to cause you to decide in my favor, I first give you an unreasonable proposition so that the choice I want you to make **appears** reasonable in contrast.

Can you tell which of the two black balls is larger? Well, if you guessed they are the same size, you are correct. It's just that the one on the left appears larger because it's seen in contrast to the smaller balls around it.

You see, we rarely gauge products or propositions in the abstract. Our assessment of value is usually made in relation to something else.

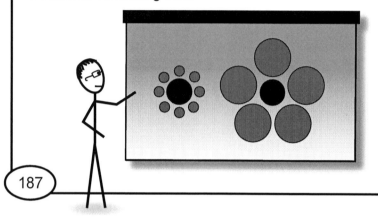

Speaking of relativity, I get a kick out of study done on CEO compensation. Back in the early 1990's not all public companies disclosed their CEO salaries. Shareholder activists thought this was wrong. The activists argued that the public should know what CEOs made – which, they believed, would keep CEO salaries in check. And so CEO salaries became public.

Want to guess what happened? Well instead of CEO salaries **declining** as a multiple of the average worker's pay, they **increased!** Want to guess why?

Because when some CEOs saw what their cohorts were making at other companies, they became quite unhappy. Many concluded that **on a relative basis** they weren't making enough. As a result the disclosures triggered a salary competition – causing a spike in CEO incomes!

"A man's satisfaction with his salary depends solely on whether he is making more than his wife's sister's husband."

H.L. Mencken

Clever marketers know how to use the principle of contrast to prod people to buy products at what seem to be very reasonable prices, at least when contrasted with other offerings.

In Billy's world, some real estate agents will deliberately show home buyers overpriced homes to make the buyer jump at the home the agent has targeted for him. These overpriced homes are decoys.

In some restaurants there are entrees on the menu which are so pricey that the proprietor never expects anyone to order them. Rather, they are there for effect – to create the impression that other items are very reasonably priced.

Please, please don't order the frogs legs.

191

"Humans rarely choose things in absolute terms. We don't have an internal value meter that tells us how much things are worth. Rather, we focus on the relative value of one thing over another, and estimate value accordingly ..."

Predictably Irrational: The Hidden Forces that Shape Our Decisions, Dan Ariely (Harper Collins, 2008)

192

There is a phenomenon similar to contrast known as **anchoring**.

The principle of anchoring states that people subconsciously work from reference points when they estimate value.

Research has shown that a persuader can influence another's thinking by first connecting him to a benchmark or reference point (an anchor).

By way of example, I would like to tell you about an experiment conducted by Professor Dan Ariely.

One day he asked his students to write down the last two digits of their social security number. He then asked students to bid on objects he offered for sale.

He wanted to determine whether anchoring the students to a number (the last two digits of their social security number) would affect how they valued (bid on) the items for sale.

And what did Professor Ariely learn?

That although the students strongly denied that their bids were affected by the digits in their social security numbers, those with high numbers bid **significantly** higher than those with low numbers.

In other words, the mere act of writing down unrelated numbers (the last two digits), created a kind of ballpark in which the students functioned when bidding on items for sale. Or, to say it another way, those students **anchored** to higher numbers were (subconsciously) inclined to bid higher amounts. Savvy persuaders understand this, of course.

195

"When a person is confronted with an uncertain situation ... the individual doesn't carefully evaluate the information, or compute the probabilities, or do much thinking at all. Instead, the decision depends on a brief list of emotions, instincts, and mental shortcuts."

How We Decide, Jonah Lehrer

196

Uh oh, time is flying.

The point I want to make is that we humans often take shortcuts in our thinking when we do not have the time, expertise or interest in making a full analysis. Clever persuaders can take advantage of these shortcuts.

All of this is a good segue for our next Rule of Persuasion.

RULE OF PERSUASION #8:

PEOPLE FOLLOW CROWDS, CELEBRITIES AND AUTHORITIES.

Many people are influenced by what psychologists call herding... they follow others in assessing the value of a particular proposition. But before we start into a discussion of herding, I want to tell you a joke.

Three lawyers are fishing. Their boat capsizes and the lawyers find themselves in shark-infested waters. To the surprise of the rescue party, there's not one scratch on the attorneys.

Any guesses?...

Yes, professional courtesy, of course!!

OK, not the funniest joke in the world, I admit. And I can tell by the silence in this room that most of you have heard better. But now let me ask you a question.

Would you have reacted differently to my joke if instead of the pin-drop silence in here, students around you started laughing out loud? Do you think that perhaps then you might have thought better of my joke? Actually smiled, or laughed a little bit yourself?

The question is not purely an academic inquiry. Rather, it is the whole point of canned laughter – that inane, fabricated and wholly transparent hee-haw you hear whenever you watch a TV sitcom.

Why in the world do TV executives think that by lacing their programs with artificial laughter, people are going to think shows are funnier than they are??

Well, here is the answer: *canned laughter works!!!*

203

Say hello to my little buddy. He's a lemming. Some people think that lemmings will follow each other into a raging river and drown. That's just a myth.

204

Lemmings are smarter than that. Sometimes, metaphorically speaking, humans not so much.

That guy's nuts!

205

An amazing phenomena of societal living is **social contagion**. This is what happens when people of all types and stripes do something because everyone else is doing it.

I first came across this term reading Professor Robert Shiller's excellent book, *Irrational Exuberance*. Professor Shiller made the point that unthinking behavior can be contagious – examples being when lots of people are buying unproven dotcom stocks or, overpriced housing **just because others are doing so**.

EEK!!

EEK!!

206

"One of the reasons we are so deceived by bubbles is the same reason that we are deceived by professional magicians. When clever persons become professionals at deceiving people, and devote years to perfecting an act, they can put seemingly impossible feats before our eyes and fool us, at least for a while. ... When we have the equivalent of professional magicians running some of our companies or acting as some of our real estate brokers, we have to expect that what we see is not reality."

Irrational Exuberance, Robert Shiller
(Doubleday, 2005)

207

Uh oh. Looks like I made a friend.

Marketers understand that people tend to follow the crowd. I am sure you have heard or seen marketing campaigns that rely on phrases like "most people prefer" or "people are switching to" our brand. This is all about getting into your head and nudging you to make a decision in favor of their product.

208

Similar to the phenomenon of crowd following or what some people call herding, there is the instinct we have to follow the lead of visible or famous people – celebrities.

When we are unsure about choices, we sometimes fall back on a reflex which tells us that if good-looking, talented people choose something, it must be good.

209

There is a series of commercials for Sony products on TV these days with Peyton Manning, quarterback for the Indianapolis Colts, and Justin Timberlake, pop star. In one of these commercials Peyton and Justin are playing ping pong.

210

Now what in the heck does Peyton Manning and Justin Timberlake playing ping pong have to do with Sony products?

Not much really. But many of us assume that if Peyton and Justin are playing ping pong in a Sony commercial, they must like Sony products. And, "heck", we think to ourselves, "if Sony is good enough for guys like Peyton and Justin, it's good enough for me."

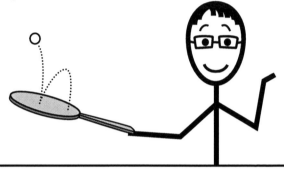

211

Now I just got a new cell phone contract with T-Mobile. I swore to my wife that it has nothing to do with their campaign featuring Catherine Zeta-Jones. I explained that I took the time to review all the different options offered by the other cell phone companies, and T-Mobile fit my needs the best.

Did Ms. Jones influence my decision? Gee, I don't think so... but, I'm not sure.

212

"A growing body of research reveals that our behavior and decision-making are influenced by an array of psychological undercurrents (unseen psychological forces), and that they are much more powerful and pervasive than most of us realize."

Sway: The Irresistible Pull of Irrational Behavior,
Ori Brafman and Rom Brafman

In addition to the weight we give to crowds and celebrities, we humans often give blind adherence to the suggestions or propositions from people who wear a mantle of knowledge, authority or success. And because of that, we are often confused when there is a disconnect between the **appearance of** knowledge, authority or success – and, the reality.

Because people often equate one's appearance with his or her integrity, insight or judgment, people sometimes follow the wrong person ... and alternatively, don't follow the lead of someone that they should.

Researchers have shown, for example, that many pedestrians at a crosswalk will follow a **well-dressed person** across the street <u>against</u> <u>traffic</u>. They just assume nice clothes ... smart guy ... knows what he is doing. **But**, put that same guy in ordinary clothing, and instruct him to cross the street against traffic, and this time he walks alone!

I am fascinated by an experiement that took place one winter day in Washington, D.C.

On January 12, 2007 – as part of a secret study – Joshua Bell, one of the most famous violinists in the world, took his $3.5 million Stradivarius violin and descended into the Washington, D.C. subway system.

And, for almost an hour he filled the subway station with some of the most beautiful music it had ever heard.

Now get this: of the 1,200 people who passed Mr. Bell that morning, only 7 stopped to listen. Most people did not even glance in his direction.

Why?

Because most of us are not able to distinguish great violin playing from ordinary violining. So, we take shortcuts: we assume that if a guy in ordinary clothes is playing in a subway with his violin case out for donations, he must be just another street musician!!

• • • • • • • • • • • • • • • • • • • •

If you'd like to see Mr. Bell playing in the subway, go to:

http://www.youtube.com/watch?v=
myq8upzJDJc&feature=related

The appearance of success or authority can also fool us in the reverse direction. In other words, we often assume that people **who appear** successful or authoritative know more than we do.

Ever heard of Nathan Handwerker? I hadn't either until I read the story of how he started **Nathan's Famous Hot Dogs**.

Handwerker was a Polish immigrant who made great hot dogs. And back in 1916, he set up a stand on Coney Island's Boardwalk selling his terrific dogs.

But, nobody was buying.

Until Nathan got an idea. He went to a nearby hospital and offered doctors free hot dogs so long as they would come to his stand wearing their white coats and stethoscopes. Nathan knew that when other hot-dog eaters saw lines of doctors at his stand, they would **presume** that his dogs were of a superior quality. And Nathan was right: when people saw the doctors in line, they jumped in behind them. By the way, we'll never know if the white-coated hot-dog lovers were really doctors or, Nathan's friends dressed to persuade.

Hey, that's not a doctor, that's my cousin, Vinny.

HOT DOGS!

We've seen how people will follow the lead of the crowd, of celebrities, and of the doctors buying Nathan's hot dogs. Knowingly or not, we humans tend to fall in line behind those who seem to know what they're doing.

Australian researchers wanted to prove that this instinct was so powerful as to influence how we experienced objective criteria – in this case, how we "see" another person.

Here's the experiment:

The researchers took a 5' 10" tall man to five different classrooms. In one classroom he was introduced as a new student. In the second classroom he was introduced as a visitor. In the third classroom he was introduced as a graduate student. In the fourth classroom he was introduced as a professor. And in the fifth classroom he was introduced as a "well-respected" professor.

The next day (the man no longer present), the researchers went back to each of the five classrooms and asked the students to estimate the man's height.

In the first three classroom, where the man had been introduced as a guest, visitor or graduate student, the students' average estimate was close to accurate – about 5'10".

Now, here's where things get really fascinating: in the fourth classroom, where the man was introduced as a professor, the estimate of his height was 6 feet tall! And in the fifth classroom, our "well-respected professor's" estimated height was 6 feet and ½ inch!

In other words, the man "grew" as his title grew!

This study shows our tendency to attribute even greater physical stature to people with a mantle of authority or success.

Now let me ask you: can you guess what type of people really understand how most of us shortcut our thinking when we are overwhelmed by appearances of authority and success?

Of course!
Con men!!

As you know, the photo on the white screen is Bernie Madoff, who ponzied $50 billion out of people's pockets.

Mr. Madoff understood the principles of persuasion.

He understood how people would bypass rational analysis in favor of presumptions of authority and success. What he offered his prospective investors was by all measures too good to be true – predictable, steady and over-market returns.

So, why did so many smart people fall for Mr. Madoff?

First, he had the presumption of authority in that he had been the head of a stock exchange, NASDAQ. Second, he had all the appearances of success – nice clothes, nice homes, memberships in fancy country clubs. Third, he employed the rules of scarcity by initially turning people away who wanted to invest with him.

And so intelligent people – letting go of their better judgment – got swayed into thinking he was the real deal.

"We are never deceived; we deceive ourselves."

Johann Wolfgang von Goethe
(1749 – 1832)

Now while a guy like Bernie Madoff was good at seducing people, he is a rank amateur when it comes to the worldwide advertising and marketing folks who compete to sell you their clients' products and services.

Next week we are going look at these businesses, review a book by Vance Packard, and learn how advertisers and marketers get inside our heads and hearts to touch our emotions.

Have a good night!

RULE OF PERSUASION #9:

DECISIONS ARE RARELY MADE LOGICALLY. USUALLY THE KEY IS ACCESSING EMOTIONS.

In preparing for next week's class I reread Vance Packard's great book, **The Hidden Persuaders**. Packard was a journalist who wrote his book in 1957.

Packard's goal was to pull back the curtain on how the advertising world played on consumers' emotions – inducing them to buy products and services. Packard made the point that shrewd advertisers and marketers create demand by pushing, pulling, or nudging consumers toward a desired emotion.

"This book is about an attempt to explore a strange and rather exotic new area of American life. It is about large-scale efforts being made, often with impressive success, to channel our unthinking habits, our purchasing decisions, and our thought processes by the use of insights gleaned from psychiatry and the social sciences. Typically these efforts take place beneath our level of awareness; so that the appeals which move us are often, in a sense, 'hidden.' The result is that many of us are being influenced and manipulated, far more than we realize, in the patterns of our everyday lives."

The Hidden Persuaders,
Vance Packard (Simon & Schuster, 1957)

233

Let me give you two examples from Packard's book.

In the early 1950's a group of companies that sold ice cream wanted to increase sales. So they hired a leading authority on consumer motivations, Dr. Ernest Dichter.

Dr. Dichter opined that the ice cream makers' advertising was boring – focusing on attributes like quality, taste and price.

234

Dichter wanted something much more exciting. Something that was more connective to the human spirit. And so he and his research team spoke to thousands of ice cream eaters.

What they learned is that to many ice cream eaters, eating ice cream was all about indulgence. It was a forget-the-calories, bury-your-face in the stuff kind of experience. Some people even used the adjective "voluptuous" when speaking about ice cream.

As a result, Dichter advised his clients to stop marketing ice cream in photos or ads showing neat scoops on sparkling plates or perfectly-shaped cones. Dichter preferred images of lavish portions of melting, gooey ice cream overflowing a plate or cone.

One of Dr. Dichter's reports suggested making ice cream appear like a liquid – to trigger the visceral, positive connection we have with fluids.

"Taking us back to our earliest sensations ... its deepest routes may lie in prenatal sensations of being surrounded by the amniotic fluid in our mother's womb."

Dichter and his researchers wanted ice cream makers to connect with people at some basic emotional level. Did his suggestions work?

Well, ice cream sales went up. And, what's more, it was about this time that **soft ice cream** became popular, and places like Dairy Queen started sprouting up all around the country.

My favorite example of how Dr. Dichter played with people's heads is the story of the prune… the lowly prune.

Back in the 1950's the prune was not very well thought of. As Packard noted, it had developed "a sort of inferiority complex." When people pondered the word "prune," they associated it with "old maid," or the phrase "dried up." What's more, the prune was considered primarily a laxative, and constipated people are just not a big market.

In other words, the interest in prunes was in the toilet.

Dr. Dichter felt that a whole new approach was needed. Somehow prune purveyors had to change the image of the prune.

239

With Dr. Dichter's guidance, the prune sellers changed their marketing. No longer was the laxative quality of the prune emphasized. And the prune's dark, murky color was deemphasized.

"In the new ads, children were shown playing ... images of youth gradually changing from children to pretty girls figure skating or playing tennis. And where prunes were shown they were in bright, gay-colored dishes ... with the pictures were jingles saying 'Put Wings on Your Feet' and 'Get That Top of the World Feeling.' One ad said 'Prunes help bring color to your blood and a glow to your face.'"

The Hidden Persuaders

240

And "lo and behold" the prunes had an amazing rebirth – prune sales spiked.

• • • • • • • • • • • • • • • • • • •

Dr. Dichter was one of the first marketers to probe **the why** of people's choices among products. Fifty years later (today), marketing people have become extremely clever about getting into our psyches with their various offerings.

If you want to persuade someone to your point of view, whatever it may be, you need to understand that the decisions people make are rarely on just an analytical, logical or dispassionate level. Rather, people make decisions at some subliminal level – some place where emotions, consciousness and logic intersect.

"Our unconscious is a powerful force. But it's fallible. It's not the case that our internal computer always shines through, instantly decoding the 'truth' of a situation. It can be thrown off, distracted, and disabled. Our instinctive reactions often have to compete with all kinds of other interests and emotions and sentiments."

Blink: The Power of Thinking without Thinking,
Malcolm Gladwell (Little, Brown, 2005)

One characteristic all great persuaders have is an ability to touch people's emotions. Salespeople, lawyers, business men and women, politicians and romancers – the great ones get it. They know that the way to influence is to reach that place in one's mind where the heart and brain connect.

Billy does not have this skill. He himself is a bit superficial and does not connect with people on an emotional level. He thinks he should be successful at real estate because people have always told him he's a smooth talker.

DREAM HOMES INTERNATIONAL

245

246

247

"Billy, the reason you don't sell more houses is because you're always thinking about what each sale does **for you**. About how large a commission **you're** going to make. About how **you are** doing as compared to others in your office. As a result, you forget that no person can persuade another unless he focuses first on **that person's needs, wants and dreams**.

"People are persuaded in their heart, Billy. You are good at presenting facts and figures. You are very articulate and polished. But, you are a robot. You do not connect with people at the level they make decisions."

248

I'm sorry that Billy took offense at what I was saying. But, I know I'm right. The key to success in moving minds is to move hearts … finding that spot in a person's emotional equation where he or she will feel safer, more attractive or more powerful by reason of your propostion. That is where persuasion lives.

249

"*MY SELLING PURPOSE* is to help people get the good **feelings** they want about what they bought and about themselves."

The One Minute Salesperson,
Spencer Johnson
(William Morrow, 1984)

250

I'm sure you realize that our making Billy a real estate agent is a **metaphor** for anyone who wants to convince or persuade another person to act or think in a specific fashion.

Whatever you are trying to convince someone to do or think, you need to keep in mind that minds are moved when the heart is moved.

251

"Reason is the slave to passion."

David Hume, Scottish philosopher (1711 – 1776)

252

OK, let's recap what we've learned so far, as we are coming round the bend to our last Rule of Persuasion.

So far we have discussed 9 Rules of Persuasion:

#1 Likeability works.

#2 Prepare. Then prepare again.

#3 Listen and watch.

#4 Scarcity pushes people to act.

#5: People want to be consistent.

#6: Create a sense of reciprocity.

#7: In lieu of analysis, people equate price and value.

#8: People follow crowds, celebrities, and authority figures.

#9: Decisions are all about emotions.

I've been doing deals for thirty years. I've done at least a thousand different deals – as a principal, a broker, or an attorney. And during those thousand deals I've seen the best and the worst of persuaders.

I've watched and learned. And I've concluded that the best persuaders – those who are consistently able to move minds – are almost always people of high integrity.

RULE OF PERSUASION #10:

PERSUASIVENESS IS ABOUT INTEGRITY.

*"If I were two-faced,
would I be wearing this one?"*

I realize that what I'm saying is a bit abstract. I understand that it's easy to spout niceties when sitting behind a desk. Of course I'm aware that in a desire to get what we want, we can be conflicted at times as to what is exactly the right way to proceed.

In fact, if you will allow a slight digression, I need to tell you about a terrible mistake I made when I was a young entrepreneur.

Early in my business life I was a real estate flipper. I would try to buy houses on the cheap and then resell them shortly thereafter for a nice profit.

So, I was always searching for houses to buy cheaply. One way to do that was to get to a seller early – right when a house was about to go on the market. I would offer the seller a quick, clean deal, and I found that many of them accepted my price, just to avoid a protracted sales effort.

One day I was in my office when I heard sirens. I was curious because sometimes sirens meant a fire, and sometimes fires meant a fire sale – in other words a house I could buy on the cheap. So I went outside to see if I could find the source of the sirens. And I did.

Just a few streets away I saw an ambulance and watched as the EMT's wheeled an elderly man out of the house. It was obvious that he had just died.

I immediately hustled to the Town Hall and learned that the man had a daughter living in the Midwest. I presumed she would know who was going to handle the sale of the house.

259

THAT EVENING, I CALLED THE DAUGHTER.

"Hi, my name is Jim Randel. I work near your father's house. I'm a real estate buyer. I was wondering who would be handling the sale of the house given his unfortunate passing. I'm a quick buyer who can save a lot of trouble in the sales process."

At first there was no response, but then I heard a soft sobbing. Then it hits me … the daughter had not yet heard about her father's death.

260

That was almost 30 years ago, and yet I still today wince when I think about what I did. In an effort to position myself to persuade the owner of that house to sell it to me, I moved so quickly that I never considered what I was doing. As a result, I ended up being the person to tell a daughter that her father had just died.

I've made many mistakes since but none has stayed with me quite as much as that one. In my rush to succeed, I lost sight of basic human compassion and decency.

You may feel that Rule of Persuasion #10 is inconsistent with what we have been discussing so far. On the one hand, I'm giving you ideas for winning a persuasion – for convincing another person to see things your way. On the other hand, I'm saying you need to be honorable in your persuasive efforts.

Of course, sometimes we face a balancing act.

The reality of any persuasive event is that one person may come out on top of the other. And, of course, I want that person to be you. Still, I think there is a way to play fair.

My presumption is that in most persuasive events, the parties involved are relatively equal in knowledge and capability. In these situations if you better the other person, so be it. What I am against are situations where:

(1) the nature of your persuasive event is such that there is a **significant imbalance** of knowledge, experience or talent between you and the person you are trying to persuade; or

(2) the result of your persuasiveness is **serious harm** to the other person.

Each of us has to determine the line between right and wrong. I cannot define what is a "significant imbalance" or, "serious harm." That's for you to decide.

My view, however, is that you can (and will) be a powerful persuader if you enter persuasive events with an overview to **play fair** and seek **win-win** situations.

"There is a third condition for persuasiveness, or salesmanship. That is the ethos, or the ethical condition of character. However other people are attracted by our apparent knowledge, however attracted to our emotional commitment ... they won't be fully persuaded unless they see us as morally trustworthy in our dealing with them.

To sell others on our projects, on our products or services, we need first to sell them on ourselves as ethical, trustworthy partners and associates."

True Success: A New Philosophy of Excellence,
Tom Morris (Putnam & Sons, 1994)

I worry about Billy's integrity. Sometimes he'll color the facts to get a prospective buyer interested in a house. That is very short sighted.

For Sale

267

One of my favorite sayings was penned by Sir Walter Scott, a Scottish poet and novelist who lived from 1771 to 1832:

> *"Oh! what a tangled web we weave*
> *When first we practice to deceive."*

I love this little poem because it's so true. People who think they are so smart that their trickery and manipulation will carry the day eventually get caught in the strands of their own web. Sooner or later (like Bernie Madoff), they end up in disgrace.

268

HONESTY IS THE BEST POLICY

1. Deceit is transparent. Most people can sense when a person is shading the truth. Often artifice backfires.

2. Even if you fool someone once, you will never do so again. And people talk. If you develop a reputation for trickiness, you will never achieve your maximum potential.

3. It takes more energy to lie than to tell the truth. Ultimately, success in anything is about an application of your limited energy in the right places. It takes creativity to be a good liar. Spend that creativity and energy in making a better (but honest) case for your position.

4. Karma: can't explain it. Have no scientific basis for it. Just believe in it. You cheat people, bad things will happen to you.

269

Sadly, we are coming to the end of our time together. I have one more lecture to give this evening to my law school class. I hear that both Billy and Beth will be there. I hope you will be as well.

270

Class, we've come to the end of our time together.

I hope you'll remember what you've learned about the art of persuasion. And I hope that you'll use your newfound skills in a manner which, while powerful and effective, will also be aboveboard and honorable.

Thanks for your attention this semester. Good night and good luck.

271

272

"Just kidding, Jim… I'm going to get into coaching. I heard about an opening for an assistant football coach at the high school and I applied. No money yet and I'll work in real estate until I can afford the transition. … Or, until Beth starts making the big bucks you lawyers make."

"I'll ignore the 'big bucks' comment … but, good for you, Billy."

"And how about you, Beth, are you sticking with a legal career?"

"Yes, of course, Jim. Coaching – schmoaching. All I care about is the big bucks!"

I'm happy for Billy. He was never really comfortable selling real estate. And by the way, for the benefit of my real estate agent friends, I want to go on the record and state that there are many honorable real estate agents out there … well, perhaps not many.

OK, enough with the humor, it's time to say good-bye. As in all of our books, I want to conclude with a summary of the 15 most important points you need to understand about the art of persuasion.

Good luck with all your persuasive efforts. And please play fair… once you develop the skills to be an effective persuader, I hope you'll use your talents in a decent and generous fashion!

15 MOST IMPORTANT POINTS TO REMEMBER ABOUT BEING A GOOD PERSUADER.

1. THE MORE PERSUASIVE YOU ARE, THE MORE LIKELY YOU WILL BE SUCCESSFUL IN WHATEVER YOUR CHOSEN ENDEAVOR.

The ability to move minds is very, very powerful.

2. PERSUASIVENESS IS A SKILL THAT CAN BE LEARNED.

By learning how people think, how they make decisions, how they communicate verbally and nonverbally, you can increase your persuasiveness.

3. YOU CAN BE PERSUASIVE WITHOUT BEING MANIPULATIVE.

At times there is a fine line between powerful persuasion and, manipulation. My rule is that you should never seek to achieve a result based on inaccurate information, a deceitful presentation or an abuse of position.

281

4. PEOPLE ARE PERSUADED BY PEOPLE THEY LIKE.

I know it sounds simple but sometimes we forget this most basic rule.

282

5. PERSUASION IS ABOUT CONNECTION.

Show the person you are trying to persuade a side of you, a common history or interest, or some facet of your personality that makes him comfortable that you are, in some ways, just like him.

6. PREPARATION IS CRITICAL.

No one thinks on her feet as well as she thinks in the quiet of her room. Consider in advance exactly what you want to achieve, how you are going to do that, how you will respond to questions or concerns, and when you will stop talking.

7. QUIET YOUR MIND. LOOK AND LISTEN.

People will often tell you what it will take to convince them. But, sometimes we miss the clues because we aren't listening as carefully as we should. Learning to read body language is also important.

8. YOU CAN PERSUADE PEOPLE BY USING THE PRINCIPLE OF SCARCITY.

People want what they can't have. One way to get people to move on your proposition is by putting a time limit on it, by limiting the number available, or by creating an aura of exclusivity.

9. YOU PERSUADE WITH NUANCE, WITH SUBTLETY.

Do not push too hard. Do not oversell. People pull back when they feel pressured.

287

10. YOU CAN PERSUADE BY USING THE LAW OF CONSISTENCY.

People can be persuaded when you put them in a position where they wish to remain consistent to prior statements or commitments. Do this in incremental steps. First get your foot in the door.

288

11. PERSUASIVENESS INCREASES WHEN YOU UNDERSTAND THE RULE OF RECIPROCITY.

People do not like to feel indebted. By creating situations where others "owe" you, you may have opportunities to employ their desire to reciprocate in your favor.

289

12. IN LIEU OF ANALYSIS, PEOPLE WILL RELY ON REFLEXES AND RULES OF THUMB TO HELP THEM MAKE DECISIONS.

When people can't easily assess value to a product or offering, they will fall back on reflexes or patterns of thinking that have worked for them in the past. One example is when people equate price with value.

290

13. PEOPLE WILL FOLLOW THE CROWD, CELEBRITIES AND AUTHORITIES.

People give credence to what the crowd is doing – if a lot of people like an offering, it must be good. When there is no crowd around, they look to guidance from celebrities and authority figures.

14. PERSUASION IS ABOUT TOUCHING SOMEONE'S EMOTIONS.

While people will tell you that they decide logically, the truth is that 90% of all decisions are made at an emotional level.

15. PERSUASION IS ABOUT INTEGRITY.

You may have some short-term hits, but your life as a persuader will be brief if you trick people ... if you lie ... if you manipulate people to make decisions against their best interest. Honesty always has been, and always will be, the best policy.

CONCLUSION

We here at **The Skinny On**™ hope you enjoyed this book. We would love to hear your comments.

My personal e-mail is jrandel@theskinnyon.com.

Warm regards,

Jim Randel

FURTHER READING

Here is a list of some of the books we reviewed in preparing *The Skinny on the Art of Persuasion*:

All Marketers are Liars, Seth Godin (Penguin, 2005)

Blink: The Power of Thinking without Thinking, Malcolm Gladwell (Little Brown, 2005)

Body Language, Julius Fast (Pocket Books, 1971)

Close for Success, Jim Londay (Longman, 1988)

Covert Persuasion: Psychological Tactics and Tricks to Win the Game, Kevin Hogan and James Speakman (Wiley, 2006)

Dirty Little Secrets: Why Buyers Can't Buy and Seller's Can't Sell, Sharon Drew Morgen (Morgen Publishing, 2009)

High Trust Selling, Todd Duncan (Thomas Nelson, 2002)

How Customers Think, Gerald Zaltman (Harvard Press, 2003)

How to Do Tricks with Cards (Collier Books, 1949)

How to Master the Art of Selling, Tom Hopkins (Warner Books, 1980)

How to Win Friends and Influence People, Dale Carnegie (Pocket Books, 1936)

How We Decide, Johan Lehrer (Houghton Mifflin, 2009)

Influence: The Psychology of Persuasion, Robert Cialdini (HarperCollins, 1984)

Irrational Exuberance, Robert Shiller (Doubleday, 2005)

Maximum Influence: The 12 Universal Laws of Power Persuasion, Kurt W. Mortensen (AMACOM, 2004)

Nudge, Thaler and Sunstein (Penguin, 2008)

People Skills, Robert Bolton (Touchstone, 1979)

Persuasion: The Art of Getting What you Want, Dave Lakhani (Wiley, 2005)

Predictably Irrational: The Hidden Forces that Shape our Decisions, Dan Ariely (HarperCollins, 2008)

Principled Persuasion: Influence with Integrity, Sell with Standards, Dr. Marlene Caroselli (CPD Press, 1999)

Real Estate Advertising, Lawrence Danks (Real Estate Education, 1983)

Sway: The Irresistible Pull of Irrational Behavior, Ori and Rom Brafman (Doubleday, 2008)

The 100 Absolutely Unbreakable Laws of Business Success, Brian Tracy (Berrett-Koehler, 2000)

The Art of Cross-Examination, Francis Wellman (Macmillian, 1903)

The Definitive Book of Body Language, Allan and Barbara Pease (Bantam, 2006)

The Greatest Salesman in the World, Og Mandino (Bantam, 1968)

The Hidden Brain, Shankar Vedantam (Spiegel & Grau, 2010)

The Hidden Persuaders, Vance Packard (Pocket Books, 1957)

The Magic of Rapport, Jerry Richardson and Joel Margolis (Hearst, 1981)

The One Minute Salesperson, Spencer Johnson (William Morrow, 1984)

The Psychology of Persuasion: How to Persuade Others to Your Way of Thinking, Kevin Hogan (Pelican, 1996)

The Power of Patience, M.J. Ryan (Random House, 2003)

The Prince, Niccolo Machiavelli (1500)

What Every Body is Saying, Joe Navarro (HarperCollins, 2008)

Why We Buy, Paco Underhill (Simon & Schuster, 1999)

Pssst ... get
the skinny on
life's most
important lessons

Remember to
visit theskinnyon.com and join
The Skinny On™ community to:

- Keep your book current
  with free web updates

- Sign up for **The Skinny On™**
  e-letter

- View upcoming topics and
  suggest areas of research
  for new titles

- Read excerpts from any of
  The Skinny On™ books

- Purchase other **The Skinny On™**
  titles

- Learn how to write for
  The Skinny On™!

Connect with us on:

www.theskinnyon.com